POETIC COGNITION

Calvin W. Allison

Calvin W. Allison
02-26-2021

authorHOUSE

AuthorHouse™
1663 Liberty Drive
Bloomington, IN 47403
www.authorhouse.com
Phone: 833-262-8899

© 2020 Calvin W. Allison. All rights reserved.
All photos taken in 2020.

No part of this book may be reproduced, stored in a retrieval system, or transmitted by any means without the written permission of the author.

Published by AuthorHouse 12/23/2020

ISBN: 978-1-6655-0572-7 (sc)
ISBN: 978-1-6655-0573-4 (e)

Print information available on the last page.

Any people depicted in stock imagery provided by Getty Images are models, and such images are being used for illustrative purposes only.
Certain stock imagery © Getty Images.

This book is printed on acid-free paper.

Because of the dynamic nature of the Internet, any web addresses or links contained in this book may have changed since publication and may no longer be valid. The views expressed in this work are solely those of the author and do not necessarily reflect the views of the publisher, and the publisher hereby disclaims any responsibility for them.

To God the Father and His Son, the Lord Jesus Christ. It was for Your glory that this book was written. Thanks for everything.

Contents

Foreword xi
The Hallways 1
Unload The Mention 3
The Midnight Of Themselves 5
The Burning Buildings Of Nostalgia 7
The Reflection's Own 8
The Good Taste Of Originality 11
Side By Side 14
Not In The Mirror 16
The Faces In The Mirror 17
Love 19
Soar Through The Storm 21
Right Here And Right Now 24
Flowers Aren't Forever 25
Don't Be A Stranger. Keep In Touch With Yourself. 26
Conclude With Respect 30
Bullseye 31
Change The Atmosphere 33
The Betrayal Of Authenticity 35
We're Paying Attention 37
Sword And Shield 38
The Mandela Effect (1) 39
The Mandela Effect (2) 40
Tendencies 41

Terrains	44
Travel With Me	46
A Hush Like Wilderness	47
Same Principle (1)	50
Same Principle (2)	51
Think About It	52
Genuine Properties	53
Life's Fires	54
Time Reflects In Moments	56
An Untamed Mind	57
In Response To A Picture Critic	58
First Impressions	59
The Genius	60
Self	66
The Equidistant	67
Not Sold	70
I'm Not A Misconception	72
To The Rescue	74
Dare You Dare?	76
The Psychological Sea	77
An Exception To The Rule	79
The Cork	80
Dreanna	82
The Right Thing	83
Modest Adventures	84
Great Things Are Ahead	85
Futures Known By Destiny	86
No Place For Gleaning	87
Think About It	88

Those Types 89
The Future 91
In Effect 92
The End Of The Rainbow 93
Expectation 94
Dietary Break Time 95
I Prefer To Be Awake 96
A Lion Of Righteousness 97
Ready, Set, Go! 98
Deciphering, "Ready, Set, Go!" 99
Travels To Destiny 102
Used To It 105
The Annals Of Endeavors 106
A Friendly Storm 108
Pensive Penny 110
Pensive Penny And Gullible Gail 111
Pensive Penny And Wishful Whitney 112
Thwart The Cruel Intentions 114
Poetic 116
Illuminated Destinies 118
Barefoot Walks 120
Enter The Exit 122
Poetic Cognition 125
About the Author 127

x

Foreword

Hi, and welcome to my newest project. Here's something to consider prior to your start into the journey that awaits you. I am regularly finding new ways to construct my thoughts into creative patterns of literature so to continually develop new ways to express myself, and even though I have written all my books while maintaining full time employment, I don't consider my writing a side job. My excessive thoughts are perpetual, and they are regularly subjected to new methods of patterning due to my severe OCD. So then how could my writing be considered a side job when my thoughts are the source of it? The two can't be in contrast because the two are simultaneous in activity. So my thoughts are my occupation and I am honored to have the opportunity to share what I have acquired from my occupation with you. I want you to see the extent that critical thinking can go and to be able to witness the nonexistent limits that regularly surface throughout the duration of this presentation. I think you'll do just fine down this road that I have paved, and I am of the opinion that you are excited about the journey ahead.

Good. Welcome, and have fun.

This way, my friends, to **Poetic Cognition.**

The Hallways

Let me stir your emotions with the touch of my pen
and I will take you to places you have not been.
I will write you a sky where your heart can soar high
as the wings in my mind enable you to fly.
No coffins allowed in the break of this day,
so let the dead die in the ground where they lay.
Keep a clear head while you enter my domain.
No tracking in clouds down the halls of my brain.
The toils in confusion get no promotions here,
so leave the milk that spoils in their barns of fear.

The mountains are cast away with the other turmoils that melted your snowmen during your relapses into retrospect where the cat of your crossings jumped through its curious hoops while the flummoxed chicken ran around a pumpkin patch until it found the dirt that no rug could conceal for the shootout on the street that subsequently became a war in a chaotic dust storm on the porch of reflection.

Let me start your engines to speed them into
a fast lane of insight they're not used to.
I'll properly place you directly in reach
of the metaphors able to help you to breach
the fathoms responsible for holding you back,
passed on from the zombies in charge of the pack.
The limits that beckon you are footprints in sand
that lead you away from your own knack to stand.
Don't let your travels be first in your ear.
It's the ones on your tongue that will adhere.

Approach me when the lame entertainments spoil your maze and I will remind you of your taste for mystery like a magnify glass in tune with translucent thoughts revealing the chords of harmony that relax the storms with intriguing hallways to walk down in order to catch a glimpse of something beyond the spoon fed hype that never sit well with the stomach of your aspirations craving originality.

Unload The Mention

Unload the mention before the dawn.
The yawn won't be gone until it's on.
The doubtful proclaim that it's a con,
but always remember the King moves the pawn.
The salt wounds the dark, and in pain it cries.
The cities are gleaning with drones and with spies.
Their shades are like monsters that hide their tries
to methodically censor their own slow demise.
Your move, adventurer. Think 10 steps ahead.
There's a valley of hope, and a valley of dread.
Be a brave knight, and use the brain in your head.
Don't be misled down the road of the dead.
Crush confusion and clear the clouded sky.
Listen to the voice that tells you to try.

The board is still there, though passing you by,
you still have the option to live or to die.
You want five dances and two coins to throw.
One for today and one for tomorrow.
But the fire escape led you to sorrow
where you couldn't pawn your heart to borrow
the rain checks that bounced, and left you in debt
in the thundering halls of striking regret.
But you've been peering through that gloomy net,
looking for something that you never could get.
And now the channel is starting to come through.
The static is breaking, and you sense something new.
The Hand that you're seeing is reaching for you.
It's time to play smart. You know what to do.

<u>The Midnight Of Themselves</u>

We escalate together through these sunsets to midnights where we ponder in the portions of the days that remain for us to analyze.

We travel in our time machines to lands of retrospect and speculations for us to evaluate and calculate the references and probable phases.

We can't fix the crooked pictures on the walls of our thoughts, but we can straighten the psychological pattern that put those pictures in place.

Reflections sometimes reveal faces that cause us to shop for masks, but the checkout is where those reflections decide how the walkout will be.

The purchases we make form our identities into the real deal or the puppets that cause laughter to break out in the cellars of captivity.

There are no receipts to be kept, but there are those purging fires that wisdom has a habit of lighting for our dark rooms that need them.

We can't fix the world, but we can individually step into it with a authenticity that allows us to witness the most beautiful sunrises

which in turn illuminates the scenery around us so that others can see something more intangible to reach for in the midnights of themselves.

The Burning Buildings
Of Nostalgia

We take journeys through the burning buildings of nostalgia only to watch frames burn around pictures we hang up in the present.

The Reflection's Own

The mirror stares. It double dares.
It shares its scares and bleeding mares.
Are you there? It doesn't care.
It knows too well that you're aware.
What a pair. What a tear.
What a flare entwined to care.
Rinse the pretense off the fence.
Condense the offense, more suspense.
Mince the expense with the whence,
hence the suspense. It's intense.
Ride or glide? Side or hide?
Open wide or say you tried?
Bleed the steed? Breed the need?
Thrash the lash till you succeed.
A double take, a triple break.
A sleeping giant now awake.
Its vision blares. It pulls up chairs.
It wears its fairs and reading tares.
It's on the attack, reflecting back
to the image about to crack.

Self-induced to be reduced.
Self-seduced to be produced
on the big screen with a dying scene
with no caffeine or a vaccine
for the sleeping teen dreaming green—
nicotine and a slot machine.
Then, before the stack of ego snacks
got smacked in their own sacks
on mental racks while the teen dreamed
of something more than what it seemed,
they awoke to the choke that broke
their mental state, and cruelly spoke
to reinstate a slowpoke joke
on a interstate with a pending stroke
to stake or break the double take
with a yoke that only jokes can make.
The laughter came with you to blame
in a game of "That's so lame."
Now the cracked mirror looks even clearer
as the terror draws ever nearer
as the dying scene leaps off the screen
like a time-machine with the teen,
who, head locked in a guillotine,
is visiting home to intervene
in hopes to find some transparency
from the crystal clear apparency.

Misguided anticipation
can be like a decapitation.
The headless horseman rides to you
with brain detached to rendezvous.
The then and now, a scary meeting.
The when and how, disturbing greeting.
Mirror, mirror on the wall,
blur old dreams, and make them fall.
Take them, break them, discard them all.
You want to answer a new call.
Don't stall. Don't follow the path back
to the dispatched heart attack.
Stand tall. Don't swallow the wrath snack
down the tarmac to the highjack.
Leave the baited hook alone.
Turn off the ringer to that phone.
Don't take an interest in that loan.
Don't be a clone with no ring-tone of your own.
Be prone to roam the guilt-free zone.
Don't fetch the bone, by the mirror thrown.
Leave it alone with its sad groan
(a tombstone on a grave unknown).
Don't postpone the gemstone able to atone.
A wind has blown in the homegrown cyclone.
The eagle has flown with wings long grown.
A lesson's been sown in the reflection's own.

The Good Taste Of Originality

Are you so cynical of being that you would devour the good taste of originality only to regurgitate a characterization unfit for the placement in the treasures of integrity?

Did you miss something as the fastball of compassion made its umpteenth pass at your bat of opportunity when you ran from, instead of took a swing at, being the hero in the field of slim pickings?

Where is the 'someday' you so often spoke of as though there was meaningful substance that should've been expectantly waited for during the electrocution of the innocents?

Perhaps hiding in a teasing corner tickling the more acceptable to gullibility while they remain victims of the charms you dangle like ripe apples from a orchard tree?

Perhaps in a scify clone that you've humorously imagined would pick up some coded torch that, though you could mimic, you never wanted to carry through the streets of longing?

Your domino effect isn't affecting in the light of positivity, but rather slamming into the standing ovations applauding morality, only, upon impact, to recoil against the pressure.

Are you so cynical of being that you would lend a cold shoulder disguised as a helping hand bent on curbing the advisory sheets that taught the straight path code of conduct?

There you go again straightening your smile to wreck another dream into the walls of your maze as you close in on another vulnerable star shining too bright for your ego to stomach.

You hold a sign that reads "Shop Here For Guidance", but dark, greedy metaphors only cut you with a tongue that has stabbed you in the back more times than you've slipped on the intellectual marbles that lie scattered on the floor.

The vents are backtracking, and though the suffocating box isn't feeding you contentment any longer, you still find ways to garner amusement from the victims that offer you retrospect in the form of your younger prisoner in the mirror.

Their hidden tears are yours to diminish like the vanquished integrity you once vaguely perceived in yourself when the music you wrote in the spontaneous concerts lit up your imagination with the dollars that sold you out.

Now you're a mere shadow puppet honking a horn in the traffic of your conscience while the parade of your dreams melts like a frozen lake that you placed your maze on while trapping yourself in the frenzy of a new same old day.

Reconciliation is only a few degrees from the mentality of your self-perception that is not so customary to pretense that it can't adapt to the climate of consideration where seemingly self-constructed proponents of rational thought wait in line to be heard.

You can find your way out if you could find your way in, and the vise versa link to that arrangement is the bridge that can enable your rationalizing with the accessibility to make a connection that can rearrange your mental disarray so that the tangible can be viewed from a first person perspective.

Then it will be up to your heart to take the lead.

Side By Side

I wish I had a dollar for every coin I made
to drop into the well that others haven't paid.
This thought to be more normal is a blur in what is real
that I can't bring into focus no matter the strong will.
I've watched your conversations and the way you interact
and have observed the mental buttons that cause you to react.
I've seen your ups and downs and have witnessed your screams.
I've taken walks around the landscapes of your dreams.
But through these course assignments, I have yet to maintain
the simplistic balance I've observed in your brain.
I've tried to keep my thoughts from the whirlwind in my mind
in order to discourse on a level more your kind.
But I just can't seem to customize a pattern to relate
the content of your intellect to the produce in my freight.
I've never been so high that I could not see the ground,
but with your naked eye I have yet to be found.
I suppose you've not exerted to any in depth degree
the mental strength that it would take to catch a glimpse of me.

But I know the waters well in which you've learned to swim,
and I sometimes like to splash in the simplicity of them.
I think you think I'm mad in the hurricanes I ride,
but you've yet to see the wind that stirs me up inside.
There's more to me than that image you often like to feed
to the preconception hogs that are too lazy to read.
If you would take the time needed to look into my heart's eyes
then you just might get captured by the sweetest surprise.
And who could say right now what you then might would see
in the entirely new world you'd discover deep in me.
Perhaps it would scare you or perhaps it would not.
Perhaps it would show you the you that you forgot.
I can't submit these files into minds that cannot hold
the reins to mental horses that ride all night to gold.
You sit in your seats while another takes the wheel,
and watch me race on by, and wonder what's the deal.
You look over at me, and I look over at you,
but we can't seem to stick to the same type of glue.
So where does that leave us, if we neither can ride?
It leaves us right here, standing side by side.

<u>Not In The Mirror</u>

Don't look in the mirror to try to find yourself.
Because you're not there.

The Faces In The Mirror

We view ourselves in these mirrors that other people hang. But the clearer we draw nearer, our presumptions become slang.
We wear our hearts like attire to blend in with the fads that turn us "outside in" with the best of the worst clads.
We stand in shades of darkness unable to get a ride from the higher class of us we've abused on the inside.
We see the smiles that hold our hearts inside of their bright hands, but we choose to noose their joyous necks for the terrorists in our lands that the hypocrites constructed to fish for their pots of gold that soon are snatched, abducted, before the hooks take hold.

The elite goats prostitute their naïve slaves to the service of their preferences while the other victims of their system run behind their weighed down u-haul trailers during the dust storms that blind them for twenty miles up the road where transparency reveals that they could have gotten there both faster and cleaner if only they had set their own pace for taste. The reflector mirror you fancied yourself being them in has become a thousand portraits of strangers who don't resemble you in any way, shape or form, and, though it's something that you have always known, it's only now, twenty miles up the road, that it's something that you are grateful for.

The tatters left for reconstructing are grateful for the alarm that alerted all your misconceptions to the dangers and the harm.
Now the ceiling is opened up and the stars are again free to journey with you once more down the path of the parted sea.
Your misinformed flashlight can be thrown into the trash, and the incorrect maps can all be burned to ash.
There was no thought too long that worked hard to correct the words that steered you wrong into a great defect.
Like scattered pieces reconnected to bring you back one truth:
it's God Who writes your whole life's book, and this page is the proof.

The ai lies become satire and the fears of polluted minds have no value to cash in at the bank of common sense. You're seeing things from an unaltered perception. What contributions do you possess to unveil in the new dawn that you have been found in? What attributes will you utilize to extinguish the flame of lies that are spreading falsehoods into hurting hearts? Are your dreams satisfied enough to put an end to materialistic ambitions? Salvation, in its proper context, is the end of all dreams because there is no greater achievement to attain. Direct your attention to your immediate surroundings and consider starting there to impart your giving.

Love

Love is not as simply put as some would like to equate it as being. It is far more complex than the verbal exaggerations that we so often hear thrown around from those aiming to garner affection. Many people use the word love to help build their image into some beaming illumination of light only to have that image rusted over through the seasons as their use of it devalues its true context disarranged by so many. But incorrect usages of it does not change its authentic meaning or sacred tone pouring constantly down upon us from the transcendental sky above. So what does love really mean then if not the clichés that trend like zany videos?

It means accepting someone without being intimidated by immediate surroundings. It means losing your own self-image of coolness that you acquired from some movie or other fabricated character of influence, and directly concentrating affection on the person to whom you make contact with without the approval of any outside source. That's right: just someone; just some random person that hasn't put a roof over your head, given you a ride, loaned you money, sat next to you in school, or benefited you in some way or another. If you can't love a random person, then you don't know what real love is. If you can't love everyone regardless of status or popularity, then you haven't got God's kind of love operational in your person. I once heard a Pastor say that he couldn't love a stranger or someone that he didn't know, to which I replied, "I can." I've known this kind of love since Christ made me a new creation. True love operates beyond the five physical senses and it is something that can't be taught, bought, or even learned. It can only be had, and identified with. If you don't have it, then you don't have it, and you can't identify with it, and everyone knows it. Yes. They know it even if they don't admit it due to its absence in their own hearts which they pretend are filled to the brim. Love can't be faked for any lengthy amount of time because the highest expectation of a person that one can have is the expectation that they will be loved by that person, and the weight of regularly meeting that high expectation through deception would be more than anyone could bear. Genuine love starts with loving God. Once you love God, ONCE YOU TRULY LOVE GOD, then you will love everyone else genuinely. There is no other way to acquire this kind of love, and it has to be a natural occurrence of opening up to reach into the supernatural realm, in which, after making contact, results in a transformation from secular to spiritual. Real love is spiritual, and unless you operate in the spiritual, you cannot know it.

<u>Soar Through The Storm</u>

The seasons baffle like rain on a snowy day
dismissing the before thought of "No way." You say
"The lightning won't strike through those transparent clouds,"
but then there is thunder in the wondering shrouds
as the deaths in your memories float up to the top
of the pictures of ventures you still cannot crop.
The lightning is frightening in the hills of your mind
where your flying of kites is a flash you can't wind.
There's no new development in the old cast away
that you found on the counter by the smoke that is gray.
Where is that thought in the season of peace?
Why did it lag if you never said "cease"?
The drought masked you over without a consent
from the leftover owner that slept in your tent.
The mirror was there reflecting your pain.
First there was mist, and then there was rain.
You wanted more coal to keep your past warm,
but the calm that you bought came with a bad storm.
A two in one deal…to play with your head.
A one of a kind… split tree that is dead.
Close up that gap and uproot that death tree
before Judas's noose becomes your decree.

Think not of yourself as a storeroom of guilt,
but rather a flower preserved to not wilt.
Stop turning a blind eye to the heart still in sight.
Make peace with yourself, and don't crash your flight.
Things aren't as hurricanic as you like to think.
So step out on the waves before you go sink.
The tornadic conditions are just in your brain.
So leave from the cellar that's kept you from gain.
Start a revolution in the season that stands.
The cost of your worth is out of your hands.
Be violent and take back the land you gave up.
The iceberg of fears wasn't meant for your cup.
Tip the thought scales that have fenced you in grief
and take down the rails that have blocked your belief.
Take that leap of faith that you've heard lots about
and soar through the storm with a thunderous shout!

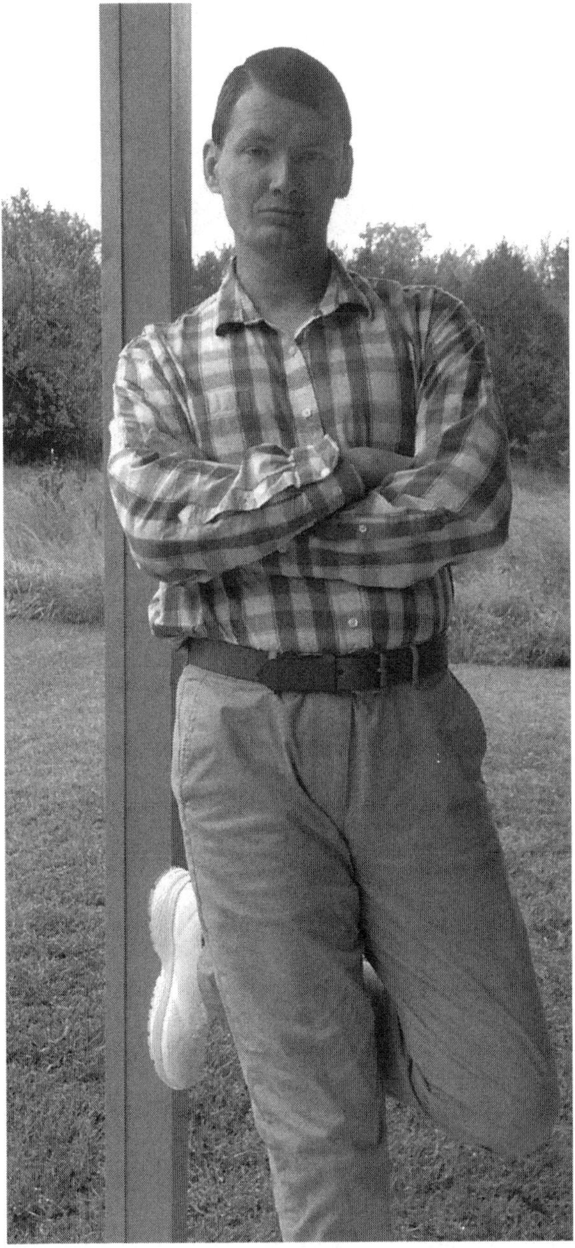

Right Here And Right Now

Right here and right now
is what determines the then
in seconds, minutes, hours,
and years from now.
Your choices develop you
into the person that you will be
and ultimately determine
where you will spend your eternity.

<u>Flowers Aren't Forever</u>

(Dietary Break Time)

Flowers aren't forever.
Neither is the pain.
The wilted stem from ashes,
and blossom in the rain.

Star lit, moon bit skies
above a rough terrain
where the shadows of their beings
find ways to remain.

<u>Don't Be A Stranger. Keep In Touch With Yourself.</u>

You want practical assessments for easy to swallow logics that repeat the same old dialogue that doesn't cross the border of your comfort zone. Yet those limits reduce your intellect until it's been self-tailored to dance with the other puppets on societies string. They (the ringleaders) have done a superb job at making you feel at home in their constraints haven't they? Their reverse-psychology arrow hit its mark precisely where they intended it to. You've become so watered down that your aspirations are just a shell of what they could be. To what extent are you content with living in the shadow that they have made for you? When you look into the psychological mirror, what reflection do you see? That of critical thinking, which allows the image of your heart to reach for expansion? Or that of textbook programming, which causes the image of your heart to default back into the box? Truth be known, many of your role-models were merely tailored to catch enough of your interest to get your money. But even though they aren't what they appear, the little hints that you've detected just don't seem significant enough to cause you to evaluate your own method of reasoning. They (your role-models) have somehow become a part of you, and their words and actions have become a representation of who you are, thus sadly ending your own originality.

Most people of influence have been scouted out by the mangy top dog elite based, not on talents alone, but also on the willingness to be scripted, cloned, or modified to carry their ideas. Ideas that oftentimes derive from the working class who strive to be seen, heard, recognized all to no avail. Instead they (the working class, yourself included) are robbed of their talents which are given to their (the top dog elite's) puppets that you cheer for and pay to play you. The coin drops into the wishing well, and your wish is manifest in the role-models that you have paid to carry your banner. An interesting phenomenon isn't it? You work for an income that you invest in a puppet who represents who you have been led to believe that you want to be. You go to school to educate yourself, and yet the knowledge that you acquire only keeps you in the box that was assembled by a scam artist that you hired (at top dollar) to build.

Blind confidence in men or women of business is a slow suicide. I took another route. I suppose seeing God for myself was a factor in my walk with Christ being, what some would call, fanatical. I further suppose that some people would call me crazy or gullible for believing things like Jesus healing the sick or raising the dead as is documented in the scriptures. Yet if someone lied to those very people and told them that a little green man from some other universe shot a green ray from a space gun into a dead person who, afterwards, came back to life, then they would believe every word. People, often times, choose what they do and do not believe based solely on how it would personally affect them. A belief in the Biblical God would mean turning from worldly pleasures and pursing a life of righteousness—which can be a very difficult pursuit/process. So, naturally, they would rather believe in a little green man who doesn't require any changes. It sounds good to the box mentality because it doesn't prompt them to leave the box that they have been designed to comfortably reside in. Turn signal activated.

The educational system wasn't designed to be of much benefit for one such as I. It was all too simplistic and my intellectual motor wasn't built for the slow lane where most traffic is content to travel. I needed more roads, more windows, more places to visit and explore. The equations that they built were like a four way stop where each time nobody knew who stopped first due to having their critical thinking paralyzed and unable to look in all directions. So it had to play out each time with the same old guess mess until you finally got to be on your way to the next four way stop with a storm added into the picture where you had to pose until you got the right shot. I was usually ticketed for playing in traffic about this time. But somehow, through all of the honking and confusion, I unintentionally picked up on just enough to get by. But where was the adventure? Where was the vividness? It was hidden in a folder stuffed in a cabinet labeled "For Real Life Usage." That's the folder that I would have selected rather than the one labeled "Early Development Strategy." But perhaps that folder would have complicated things even more so for the majority who did benefit from that strategy. I've never been completely against the educational system, but I've never been completely for it either. So where does that logic reside?—in relevance to the receiver. If it works for you, then it's good for you. But it's not a one size fits all. Some course designers simply don't have the capability to modify exact fit strategies onto certain intellectual shapes and sizes. Originality is the key here, the punchline to all of this (redundant to me) assessing and equating that I implore you to embrace or at the very least consider. What are you if not original?—a willingly stringed puppet purposed for servitude? A recipient of no authentic love or gratitude from a system that you personally chauffeur around to mental hotels so it can continue to draft/catch new graduates, flay and serve them (sometimes as an appetizer, depending on how well they followed the recipe) to its clientele? Is that who you really want to be, and is that what you really want to do? Who are you after critical thinking? Think about it, and then get back in touch with yourself.

Conclude With Respect

Leveraged by dark echoes, the guilt surpasses
the confidence that grounds the heart in hope.
The regrets become monsters that bite at
every pure idea, making it hard to cope.
The voices clash as renegade dreams make
the mind feel crazy in its war zone of thoughts.
The doubts have all been collapsed, but
glimmering still are the wayward rogue dots.

The times of recognizing the threat have long
passed in the shower of recycled retrospect.
The stage has been set for the reflect net
to catch its subjects to dissect each aspect.
But how long are the longing halls where
wind and fire repeat their ransom calls?
Can the redial thwart the barroom brawls
where blood stained hands built their walls?

Certain matters lie unattended as ended
as the bright sword's sharp deadly point.
Sometimes releasing that end is the only
shot at getting a grip that won't disappoint.
The rogue dots must be scattered into the
new dawned sky before they can connect.
Then the puzzle of life will reveal a new picture
that the heart can conclude with respect.

Bullseye

You're sinking in a field where you dislocated sight.
Thinking with no yield through the briefing on goodnight.
The stars are like police that you deputized to chase
the dreams that did not cease to forfeit every race.
So now you're on the bench, wanton and forbearing
with tears that work to drench the wings that lifted daring.
Fearful are the thoughts that have yet to transpire
into the bullseye shots that never got to fire.
The portal to your gold closed inside of your head
where you fought the day to hold the night that made your bed.
You spent your time on coupons that caught the early worm
running from the crayons that portrayed it as a germ.
The rainbows were your spills that hooked you like a fish.
You threw your lines like bills that focused on the dish.
The signal came in clear, unlike your static goals
that caught on to your sneer, but never to the coals.
Your coloring was bland in outlines of mirages
where the hats on the stand unleashed their cruel barrages.
You fought hard to maintain a balance in each role,
but the ape inside your brain was the one that took control.

So logic is on trial as it pertains to you.
The verdict's not in style, but you know that it is true.
Coincidence has no part in anything at all.
There's no ape inside your heart, that idea has got to fall.
There's cause and there's effect, and a guided design.
You've learned from retrospect, and now you're feeling fine.
The shot has been fired, and your wings lift to fly.
Look at what's transpired, it's a narrow bullseye.

Change The Atmosphere

Modify the metaphorical until it's historical.
Mount the cannons on the mundane wall.
Shoot them off in a evening spectacle.
Place the dots and connect them all.

Cross over a leg and chase the stars.
Lift your eyes to the poet's sky.
Break your mentality out of the bars.
Teach your identity how to fly.

Tailor your visual to fit the impossible.
Prompt your heart to take a leap
with handfuls of thoughts that are compossible
with dreams that exist outside of your sleep.

Move beyond the temporal domains.
See existence from a new perspective.
Kill all your doubts and leave their remains
outside the realm of retrospective.

Stare down the weapons aimed at your head.
Don't get triggered by envious looks.
Live to your fullest among the dead
who can't interpret the lines in your books.

Sail with the ships that others can't see
on oceans that they cannot perceive.
Step back from the A and onto the Z.
Return to the sender, delete to receive.

The Betrayal Of Authenticity

We travel great distances to see ourselves in the mirror only to be shattered in the reflection of preconceptions that others have drowned us in time and time again.

These deaths hold no value to the one's who cheat lives out of existence, draining them into the dead realm of hypocrisy wherein lies no authenticity.

Both the cheater and the cheated are one in the same only differing in the chronological order of circumstance that is relevant in accordance with vain expectations.

We fancy a fictitious personality that we admire to the extent of betrayal of our closest friends in order to photoshop some invented stranger in their rightful place.

We say "just be yourself" with a lying tongue so that we can shoot them down the instant they break character and try to be someone that we're not—themselves.

We taint the sacred heart, and stain the merits of oddity by shaming the unmasked face that screams to be noticed in the social cesspool society deems acceptable.

The deep waters swallow us who feign an inability to swim, tailoring our reflections to fit the slimy surface that we've chosen to collectively gather ourselves by.

We secretly play marco-polo with shallow remnants of thoughts standing in remembrances of principles we surrendered to the tyrants who thought we were stars.

I say "we" in reference to a humanity that I once tried identifying with only to be shut out, beat down, and killed by as their self-censored pool games became visions of myself.

What is so wrong with authenticity that you would go to such measures to ridicule, with your exaggerated tones of self-importance, its prestige and grandeur?

You esteem yourselves to be kings and queens in a giant coffin where maggots and worms feast on your embellished value seen with eyes full of dirt.

By what authority, other than your own, do you decree yourselves to be so exquisite that you would deny the wondrous nature of honesty that threatens your fiendish ambitions?

The stones you are throwing are becoming walls around your slimy pool that is actually a swamp filled with crocodiles in observance of your trespassing mentality.

To what will you attribute your nakedness when the attire of your fantasies cease to adorn your mental body in the ill lit dawning of abrupt transparency?

Will you then be as you are now scattered in a maze of characteristics hoping to find the one that would establish your counterfeit persona on the walls of illegitimate legitimacy?

I think not, oh lost star, frozen like the tongue that recited its last script only to realize it was first a biography before it was a fantasy mirroring its disconnected self.

You will surrender or die, and the clouds above the forest will still produce a rain that will fall on a world where only a few find the right soil to plant themselves in and grow.

We're Paying Attention

Most people in the public eye fail to understand that many of us listen very closely to what they are saying in order to determine if their views are sincere or just empty words recited from the mouth of a puppet acting on the strings of popular demand. The majority of the general public are absolutely fine with a puppet and won't question conflicting views that transition with the status quo seasons. But there are many of us still who admire authenticity even if that authenticity conflicts with our own views. But we, that many, connect on a profound (almost complex) personal level with those who's authentic views align with our own, and on that level there is a mutual admiration one for another.

Sword And Shield

We write in fields where the storms entertain
a traffic that yields to swarms in the brain.
The windshields of time reveal a bookstore
like a compass of valor that points to a four-
way go light that is designed to stay green
unlike all the grime on the robotic screen
where inspiration is so often tainted
and motivation is so often painted
with brushes that muzzle the dogs in the back
who bark at the wolves who like to attack.
But our pens are like shouts sending out an alert
that breaks through the censors they like to insert.
We travel the distance that others can't go
to bring them the sun that shines in the snow.
We build inward snowmen to keep them aware
of the scarecrows in fields who blow their hot air.
We want all the crows to eat with the eagles
while tigers and lions play chess with the beagles.
We exclude no one in our invitation
to ride on the waves of inspiration.
We scare off no one with our noble tactics
to saddle round tables with graphic didactics
designed to form concepts that turn dreams to gold
at the end of the cross bow where arrows aren't tolled.
The directions are free, through the storms that won't yield,
to a traffic at sea who seek sword and shield.

The Mandela Effect (1)

The Mandela Effect is easily explainable, and it's not the work of a alternate universe. It basically consists of false information presented from media or rumors, misstated quotes by popular persons, which in turn are repeated by the public resulting in the misstated quotes gaining wide spread notability, and people thinking movie depictions are always historically accurate. That about sums it up.

<u>The Mandela Effect (2)</u>

The Mandela Effect is a classic case of, what I call, LAZY RATIONALIZING. Easily explainable, yet people just want something so badly to be intrigued by that they are willing to toy with their mentalities. Like when people see a animal in the evening running across a field and trick themselves into believing that it could have been the mythical Sasquatch. LAZY RATIONALIZING.

<u>Tendencies</u>

We see ourselves in turmoil inside a closet of doom,
hoping to drift into a spoil that won't soon consume the broom.
We need our slates removed from where they like to hide,
but our lights are not approved for that kind of Son lit ride.
So we take the dots that spill rather than to connect,
and color them with our will that we try all life to eject.
Usher in these roller coasters that track the scoop on down,
and tear up the controller posters that paint dignity like a clown.
Sugarcoat no disaster that opens us up to more
of less a shot at faster travels to lands we've crashed before.
Our smiles are not forgotten in the plagues that made us stem
from the ashes of the rotten fruit that we ate then from them.
Tend not to these obituaries that tell of our sad dead dreams.
Let the weeds hide those mortuaries embedded in all those screams.

The kites have flown from yesteryear and the stars have watched them die
in the places of our deepest fear where the future waves goodbye.
So into this deeper void do we throw our trash away
as the times that we enjoyed show us how to keep the stay.
And here we stand, still guarded, by the shield that is secure.
The sea has roared and parted while the lighthouse kept it pure.

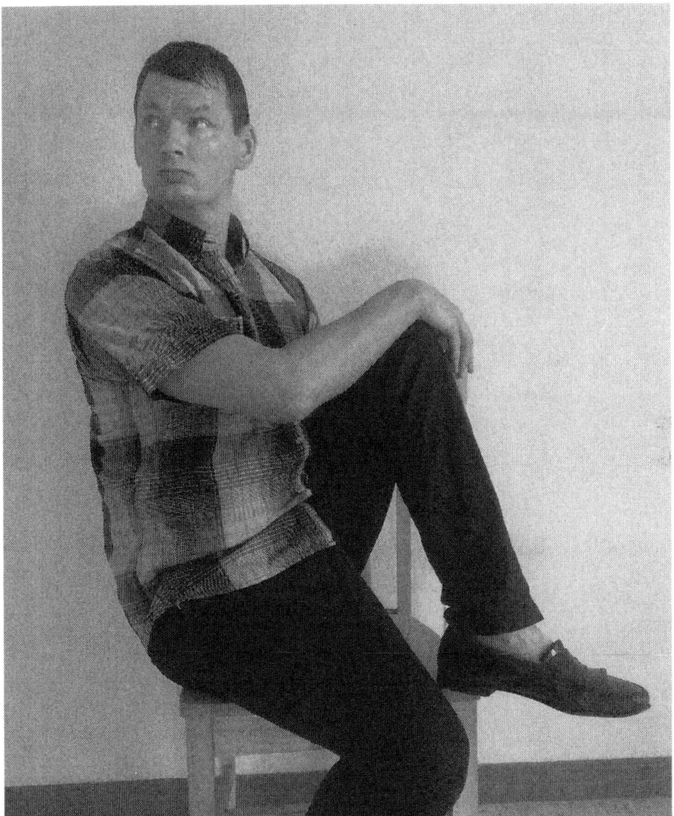

Terrains

Wearing loafers in the rain
is not the best use of the brain.
Yet still the clock remains
and the universe sustains.

So I walk the social drain
like a magnet for disdain
over nets in alley lanes
set by clumsy hurry canes

who trip on their own gain
and crash into the plain
who share their labor pains
unaware that they are chains.

I do not catch their train
or fall for their campaign.
Like a lion with no reigns,
I roam through mad great Danes;

both the rabid and the vain,
the morbid and insane,
who profit from profanes
outsourced from their domains.

To what does it pertain
to go against the grain
when the stain of 'heart remains'
stains one's moral gains?

That thought tends to sprain
their desire to retain
the knowledge that explains
how not to get in skeins.

Take heed, you hasty crane,
lest you buckle from the strain.
The bent are bent on feigns
to lure you from your wains.

And I move in my drenched twain
as one they can't detain.
As one who just maintains
regardless of terrains.

Travel With Me

Travel with me on the edge where moments are experienced to their full capacity.
Where the bright winds move about lifting hopes that spread fires throughout the land.

The clock ticks and you are caught in the minute.
Your demeaning faces can no longer hide themselves.
Your good deeds are poisonous like cyanide.
Your jealous punches are weak attempts for adoration.
But who now will hold your mask?
Who will watch the door as you beat your fellow man?
Your smile is wicked and your haughty attitude has taken you down with the ship.
Your crooked ways have found you out,
and your ties reek of corruption.
Your sweet words melt like ice in a glass that nobody wants to drink from.
Your pleasantries are rotten reflecting from your own deceitful heart, and the clock still ticks. Tick Tock. Tick Tock.
The hour strikes, and you are old in your decrepit bed trying to find some cover to hide your face from a world that sees.

<u>A Hush Like Wilderness</u>

You missed the point.
You didn't catch the view.
What were you expecting?
A I.O.U. ?
You walked the thin ice
until it broke.
Then all of your dreams
went up in smoke.
You drank to the song
that played you at night,
and went with the wrong
that said "It's alright".
Like a wrinkled tea-shirt,
you spilled on your ice,
then went to the bottom
to get your advice.
You're thought-deep in guck.
Your hands are tied.
Your feet are both stuck
in the tongue that lied.
A star is falling
out of your mind
into your heart's sea
where you went blind.

Fuzzy feelies
are awfully silent.
Silly pun 'reallys'
are looking violent.
Those crooked stares
that you get on the wall
hurt even more
when you don't get a call.

A hush like wilderness appears.
A rush like tenderness adheres.
Leaves are falling from a tree
that you didn't expect to see.
Distilled the toxic days become
for just a moment, chewed like gum.
Then the baggage jumps back on.
"Chew on that!" taunts the carillon.
Your bell got rung and drowned out your tune.
The trapdoor sprung and burst your balloon.
Silly rabbits are eating your cereal.
Your battery's dying because it's material.
You've made your bed, but you don't want to climb in.
You're dying to live, but you can't pull the pin.
The guilt is attacking from every side,
steering your wheel down a road broke and wide.
Yet there's one narrow road that, if you'd just take,
would take you to make, and not to break.

So break from yourself, and go to the cross
where many before you found in their loss
a new birth of life. This is your cue.
Catch the view of this point, and not deja-vu.
Choose life or choose death. It's all up to you.
Tick-Tock. Tick-Tock. 5.4.3.2..........

Same Principle (1)

Seeing a grown man afraid of ai is like seeing a kid who hasn't yet learned that pro wrestling is fake.

Same Principle (2)

Hearing Hollywood liberals trying to deter people from climbing the capitalistic ladder of success is like listening to a group of drunks telling people not to drink.

__Think About It__

Here's something to consider: let's say that you spent hours upon hours upon hours drawing a work of art that would become your masterpiece. Consider all of the time and effort it would take to design and get every detail exactly right. Then think about how ecstatic you would be, the exhilaration you would feel, upon its completion.

Now then, after all of the time and hard work that you put into that project, how would you like it if someone came along and scribbled on it? How would that make you feel? Okay, considering that, how do you suppose it makes God feel when someone gets a tattoo?

<u>Genuine Properties</u>

If we consider the many facets of intellectual spheres, then we can conclude in terms of genuine properties. Tailored as many may be to fit into a persona of influence, the authentic liberty still pertains, persisting to their individual attributions. There are no disguises for thoughts. They are already hidden from those to who they do not belong. No two minds think exactly alike, and it is in that logic that a unique canvas for each life resides.

<u>Life's Fires</u>

We latch on to material things
as if they have some golden wings
that can fly us to a happy place
where dreams reach out and touch our face.
Where warm vibes veto inward insights
that try to tend to the trailing taillights
on the vehicle of neglect
that we feign to not detect
while our hearts work to correct
the root cause of this defect.
The temporary leaves us stationary
in the ordinary of what's momentary.
But our hearts sense something more
than goods in a temporal store.
They long for spiritual inductance
to fight off the flesh's reluctance
to let go of tainted desires
or to kindle perpetual fires.
The backwards gets us grooving
until we see it moving
with its cruel consequences
and its ruthless recompenses
sabotaging self-structured security,
silencing suppositions supposing surety.
Quicksand isn't a foundation of rock.
It's a time bomb, "Tick-tock. Tick-tock."

Soldiers sinking, Sergeants shrinking
in the offices of shrinks, drinking
their thoughts with dot kinks, not blinking
though ought to be turning, or caught thinking,
and not by surprise as though in disguise
of an intellectual not in their size.
Dot kinks can't be connected,
but they can be inspected
once they've been detected,
and then can be ejected.
We struggle too often with kinks
as we copy their broken links
that paste us in choking syncs
where a mind too often sinks.
The poison is not a cure
no matter the strong allure.
It's only when hearts can endure
that life's fires can make them pure.

<u>Time Reflects In Moments</u>

Time reflects in moments of understanding.
Blueprints to the construction of productiveness.
Instructions detailed in the mental ink of
contrasting retrospect recycled for success.

An Untamed Mind

For several years I tried hard to convince myself that others thought as I did. But, after a great deal of evaluating their methods of reasoning, I slowly began to realize just how different we rationalized. They mostly seem simplistic, and, as much as I have tried, I just can't reason in that, or in a likewise, manner. I admire simplicity though, and there is grandeur in it that is attractive. But I have a wild, untamed mind with loud, vivid thoughts that can't seem to settle in one moment. My moments regularly collide together resounding in the next and in the next and in the next. I take comfort in knowing that I was designed like this, and that I'm only different here in the temporal. God completely understands me, and He has set my purpose into motion. In His great Hands I reside.

<u>In Response To A Picture Critic</u>

I'm actually a very joyful person. But being a genius with a photographic memory mixed with a strong case of OCD makes for a difficult picture sometimes.

First Impressions

First impressions don't mean much to me. It's usually about the fifth that catches my attention.

<u>**The Genius**</u>

Many people are accustomed to having misconceptions about geniuses, so, being a genius myself, I would like to disclose some insights to possibly help with understanding us a little bit better. Contrary to what is generally thought, we don't know everything, but we do know a lot. We have an ability to perceive things that most people aren't able to, and since our intelligence is higher than the majority of others, it's only natural that our behavior is different. The first thing to look for in a genius is odd behavior.

I was around 40 years old when I recognized my own oddity in character, and I was completely caught off guard by this transparency. I had been aware of my very difficult mental battles, such as OCD and Misophonia (though for several years I didn't even know they were actual conditions), but I convinced myself that those were basically just issues that weren't actually attached to my character. I thought that I could confine them to my private life, and that the world around me wouldn't be able to detect them, and I convinced myself that the majority of others probably went through similar things. But I was wrong. My conditions were not normal, and I was not normal. Upon this realization, I told a longtime friend that I had come to the realization that I was different from everyone else, to which he replied, "I've always known that."

At around the age of 16, while in Geography class, I learned that I was a speed reader by simply trying to get through the portion of textbook that my teacher had called on me to read. The class was astounded that their quiet, disconnected classmate could read as clear and as fast as he could, and I was a bit astounded by this as well. I had never tried to read fast up until that point.

I was around the age of 16 or 17 when I discovered my ability to write poetry. I was sitting in ISS (In School Suspension) and was dealing with the aftereffects of a tough bout with manic depression when I started writing down some of my feelings. Those descriptive feelings manifest into a 16 line poem that the teacher snatched out of my hand immediately after I finished writing it. The teacher took the poem to the principal who called me into his office. After I assured him that the poem was merely expressing my feelings, he asked me something that had a profound effect on my life. He asked me, "How can someone with the grades that you have write something this well?" I had never taken school very seriously, and I just did enough of the assignments to keep the teachers off of my back. So that lack of interest manifest into low grades. The school system had basically written me off as an unintelligent student with a learning deficiency, and the negative views that others had of me eventually had an influence on how I perceived myself, which was negatively. That's the backdrop for the context of the Principal's question.

I had never really given much thought about my intellectual capabilities until that day in the Principal's office when that question was put forth. My poetry not only changed the perspective that I had of myself, but it also changed the school's perspectives of me, and teachers and students alike began requesting more and more of my poems to read.

It was also around the age of 17 when I learned that I had a photographic memory. I discovered this while my dad was teaching me how to play the guitar. Being an expert guitarist, he was amazed at how quickly I could learn the songs that he was showing me how to play and it was at that time I realized that I had the ability to retain any information that I desired.

I can read whole lines in a single second or less, I can often read people's thoughts, I can hear a large room of people talking at once and am able to distinguish the voices, I have performed telekinesis on occasion, I can remember anything I choose to lock in my memory and sometimes things I don't choose to, I have vivid memories of my life before I was one year old (like the time my sister got attacked by a dog on third street or the time I swallowed a baby rattler and almost died), I can usually control my dreams, my imagination looks as real as reality to me (but I never confuse the two), I have occasionally been able to see detailed events before they happen, I have written whole poems in my head before writing them down on paper, I have to pattern my thoughts in order for me to escape the compulsions that cause me to repeat actions (the systematic patternization of my thoughts assists me in maintaining both a private and public life), and so forth and so forth.

I could go on and on about my mental abilities, and about the mental battles that I have faced and still am facing, but I would like to move on to something else.

I enjoy watching documentaries of other geniuses because of the particular way that I can relate to them. Meaning we share similar intellectual spheres that are not common in the general society.

People like Bobby Fischer, Howard Hughes, Nikola Tesla, Albert Einstein, Edgar Allan Poe and other genuine geniuses are all people who have characteristics that I can identify with to some degree.

Many people who are reported to be geniuses in the technological era of the 21st century simply aren't. Many so-called geniuses have merely merged their ideas with the ideas of others who have already established themselves as genuine geniuses so that they can blend in with the genius label. They get credited for some outstanding achievement when all they really did was hitch a ride with the origin of the achievement. Some so-called geniuses have had their careers, or legacies, financed by corrupt entrepreneurs who turn them into puppets so that they can push political agendas on a unsuspecting society.

I prefer not to bring up my IQ test results because the results are susceptible to change if one decides to take the test again. But, out of regard for the clarity of this article, I'll concede my reservations. My score showed that I had a IQ of 144, which means that I am in the highest 1% bracket, however, I believe that I could score higher than 144 if I were to undergo more testing.

Are IQ tests a valid determining of intelligence?—to some degree they are, and to some degree they are not. Passion isn't tested in a IQ test and things that people aren't passionate about are typically harder for them to learn. For example, I have little interest in automotive mechanics, and therefore probably couldn't be a career mechanic. But there is something to be said about the intellectual capabilities of a knowledgeable skilled mechanic who knows all the details of a vehicle's operations. While a genius may have a much larger intellectual circumference than that of a basic mechanic, the mechanic basically has an equivalent IQ to the genius in the particular area of their trade. We are all programmed differently.

I am completely aware that God has given me my mind, and that all of the knowledge that I possess has merely been installed in me by Him. I don't view myself as special, but only as different, and that difference, that designed set of characteristics are there to bring about God's purpose for my life.

Well, I suppose that about sums it up. I hope that this article has helped bring more understanding to the topic on what it really means to be a genius. Thanks for reading, and always remember to keep an open mind when viewing the world around you.

<u>Self</u>

Have you ever noticed anything about someone that you wished wasn't like it was? If so, did you ever stop to think that what it might quite possibly be is that you're not very understanding, caring, patient, friendly, or loving?

<u>The Equidistant</u>

I can see the point A and I can see the point Z,
but the point M to me is a mystery.
Point L had its say, and point N strolls a sea,
but point M remains a mystery.
I circulate the colors of each detail,
and associate the numbers with their tale,
and perambulate the circumference
to reach the inference,
but still the equidistant has its veil.

I can see the point A and I can see the point Z,
but the point M is clearly a monopoly,
dictating point A and dictating point Z
by random factors of relevancy.
I condensate the fabrics of each design,
and irrigate the graphics to entwine,
and affiliate the topographic
with the mental aspect,
but still the equidistant won't headline.

I can see the point A and I can see the point Z,
but the point M is surely of metrology,
assessing the point A and surveying the point Z
in the maze of all its mystery.
I cogitate on files in the drawer,
and calibrate the styles still in store,
and correlate the stockpiles
with the textiles,
but, veiled, the equidistant keeps offshore!

I can see the point A and I can see the point Z,
but the point M to me is a mystery.
Point I had its say, and point Q strolls a sea,
but point M remains a mystery.
I crenellate the lesson from each trial,
and designate a session for each mile,
and coordinate the lessons
with the sessions,
but the equidistant has no dial.

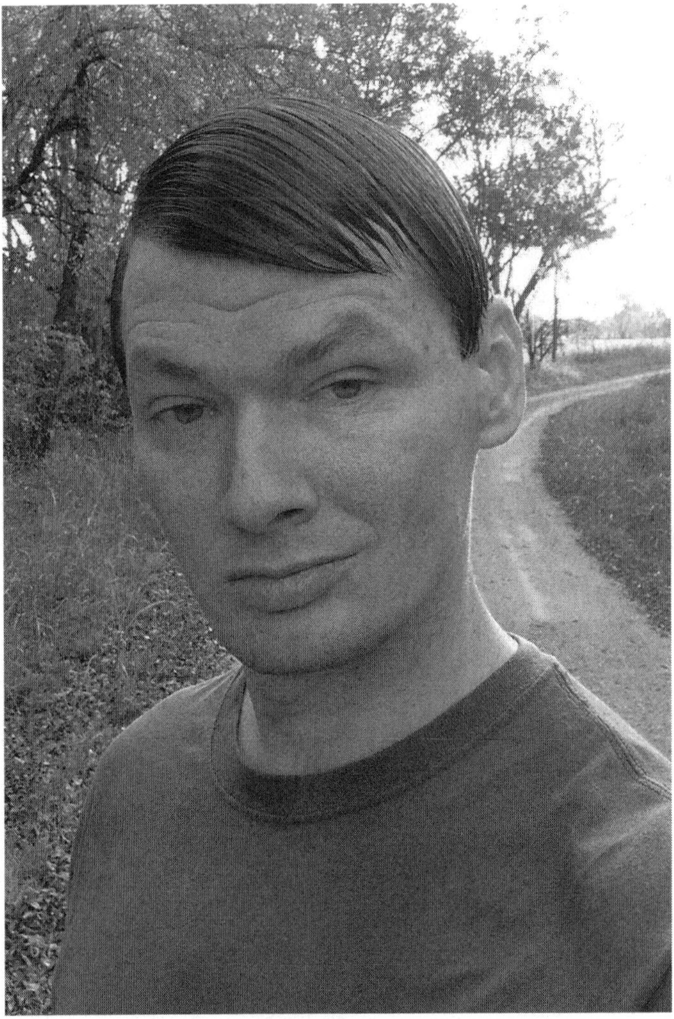

<u>Not Sold</u>

They look me over from a distance
and wonder why the resistance.
They kindly offered their assistance,
but I refused in that instance.
I'm a puzzle it would seem
and one that makes them scream.
Oh if only I would deem
to not be so extreme.
"Then," they say, "we could work together,
kick up a storm, enjoy the weather.
Flock together as birds of a feather."
I roll my eyes with a big "Whatever."
"Be like us," they say, "and water it down.
That fire of yours could burn down the town.
What do you say, plural or noun?"
"I say you're a sellout, a fraud, and a clown."
So I stand apart from the crowd
peering through their deep dark cloud
right through their masks they've self-endowed,
as their sneering grows more loud.

They want me to be all that I can be
as long as I star on their T.V.
A poster boy wingman to say "That's right".
A puppet on a string man to stay within sight.
No oddity of character, no mind in free mode,
just a 'yes man' tin man on their yellow brick road.
Not sold!

I'm Not A Misconception

I'm no coward behind a mask with no face to be worn by your tendencies to be gullibly wrong in your shade of synthetic tree where you are delighted to play the victim in another script wherein the writer, unknown to yourself, wrote your part so accurately precise that the precision has you shaking in your familiar reflection reflecting the face that was always your habit of unfolding once out of the drawer where your favorite pretenses are kept.

You straighten out the day as though it were wrinkled and try to mold the clay as though you were sprinkled with some magical dust that makes your fallacies pure rather than just dingy rust with no charm or allure except for in the notion that you felt right to conceive, like a self-righteous potion that you chose yourself to weave,
that the deep web of lies is just a new neat fad,
but the spider in your eyes reveals that you've been had.

I'm no naïve bottom feeder waiting for a morsel from your vomit to be tracked in on my clean carpet where the dots are not obstructed and are able to be connected like trillions of light-bulbs that you can't see due to your self-eclipsed nightlight that you installed to mimic a scarecrow of sort in a field of truth where your spider eyes don't want to crawl for fear of exposing the cowardly hypocrite behind the mask that's unable to conceal your identity.

You sink into the stars to wish them all away
while thinking in your bars to squish away the day
so plainly there to reveal the path that you need to take,
but there's pleasure in your zeal for romancing what is fake,
and in that poisonous stance, you remain in a hyped cell
where you stood so to advance in the places that you fell
only to fall again with a laughter on the face
of the mask that wore you in while it fits you back in place.

To The Rescue

There's a damsel in distress.
She's shaking in her heels.
She's gotten in a mess
and hates the way it feels.

Her eyes are big with fear.
Her mouth is opened wide.
She's bound to a chair
with a villain on each side.

So much for pretty smiles
and her woman's intuition.
She needs help and needs it fast
before her demolition.

Well it just so happens
that I'm a masculine man,
and if I can't do it,
then nobody can.

So, baby, hold on tight.
'Cause I'm on my way.
It's gonna be alright,
I'm gonna save the day.

I rush onto the scene
and I just do my thing.
I've got a swing in my step
and a step in my swing.

I untie the cutie pie,
and then sweep her off her feet.
Yeah, I'm the type of guy
to get you out of your seat.

I take the heat to the street,
and I don't skip a beat.
Yeah, I'm the type of guy
to get you out of your seat.
I'm just the type of guy
to get you out of your seat.

Dare You Dare?

Dare you dare to spare your share
of guilt induced you deem to bear?
Why go ye to all the trouble
to order double of that rubble?
It's not your cup to fill it up.
A sip, a drink, a store holdup.
What's in store is more and more
of the first shot of the war, the fore
that you abhor to adore
in a hard downpour on your floor
where your wings can't lift to soar
above the store where "wear" isn't "wore."
And so you wear the tear and bear the stare
that you shop there for
instead of saying "no more delaying"
and closing that door
to the room that resumes to consume
as you resume to mop its floor.
Yet "It is finished." It is no more.
The price has been paid, the brick work laid
for a brand new incorruptible, indestructible store.
A golden shore forevermore.

The Psychological Sea

When mental oars won't row,
step out onto the flow.
Walk the sea in your mind.
Don't let the storm make you blind.
Maintain focus, calm your thoughts.
Work it out. Connect the dots.
Get a grip. Hold on tight.
Aim your heart at the Light.
Shoot out from the box.
Be unorthodox.
Keep yourself from sinking.
Direct your thinking.
Dismiss the loud crowds.
Push back the dark clouds.
Penetrate concentration.
Anticipate penetration.
And there you'll be once again
safe on the shore with the win.

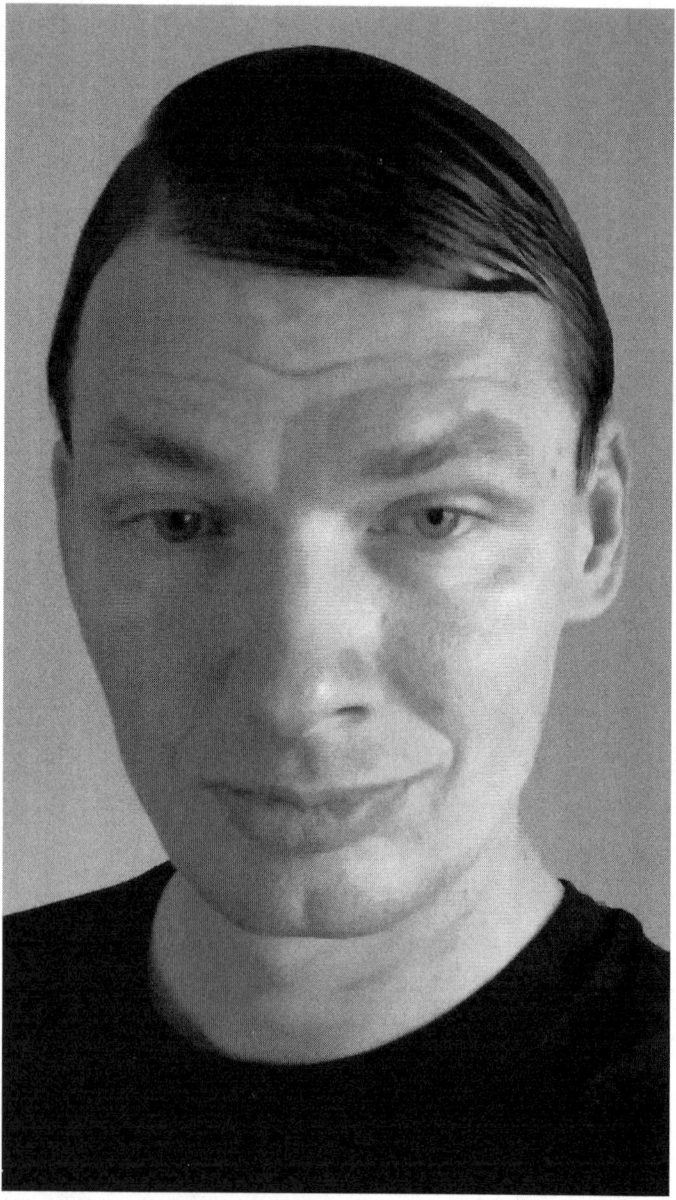

An Exception To The Rule

I've heard it expressed before that a writer should read a lot in order to gain insights from experienced or professional others, thus following the general blueprint of the long chain of authors. Well, I guess that I'm a bit odd or a bit unorthodox in that chain, because I just don't read many books. Don't get me wrong, I've read the Bible from cover to cover more than once, and I stay diligent in my studies, and research, I just don't read many books by modern day authors.

The Cork

(For The Quiet Librarian. Stasia.)

I cast my line, but you don't take the bait.
I cross over a leg as I sit and wait.
I caught a glimpse, but the glimpse wasn't fair.
I want to touch your soft face and hair.
I want to take you by a delicate hand
and lead your heart through the poet's land.
I want to show you many wondrous things
in heights reached only with poetic wings.
They say there are many fish in the sea,
but you're the one I would like it to be.
Breathe with me in this unveiled sunrise
and let me sweep you into surprise.
I'm yours for the taking, a heartbeat away.
Slay me, flay me, in sweet disarray.
Let me break through the walls that you built
to tend to the rose you don't want to wilt.
Let me inside the door that you guard
to see the card you wouldn't discard.
Your essence would blossom in my keep and care,
and your smile flourish, oh, maiden so fair.
Poetically tailored each moment would be
of you pressing in to the embrace from me.

Your feminine package I'd handle with care
in so fragile of manner on voyages we'd dare.
Catch fire with me in a dark world of night.
Allow me to pilot your life's greatest flight.
It'd be happy travels through thick and through thin.
The nest of the blest is the best Royal Inn.
Reveal the mystery that leads me to you
and I will be there like a mornings new dew.
Layout a map that shows the whole route
and I will arrive with a victory shout.
The envelope's stamped, you just have to mail it.
I've pulled out the chair, you just have to come sit.
The ocean of romance has a place for us
where there's no such thing as superfluous.
Ride this wave without saddle or bridle.
Be valiant, brave. It's a groundbreaking tidal
coming in to shore to reach for your hand.
Step onto this water as though it were land.

Dreanna

So who is this Dreanna, about whom I write?
She's a girl worth some time in the poet's spotlight.
Dreanna is sweet and knows well how to style
a nice meet and greet with her radiant smile.
She's neat and polite, courteous and pretty.
Upbeat, not uptight, but vivacious and witty.
A hard worker, a mother whose heart is all there.
A warrior, convivial, a treasure that's rare.
Dreanna is kind to an unusual degree.
A petite little rascal I look forward to see.
A spunky ball of fire who's all over the place.
A bubbly doll live wire who sets her own pace.
Her hair as black as night. Her face as bright as day.
Her abruptness in expression a spectacular display.
Her feminine posture, and intellectual brew
make quite the quaint package, from my point of view.

<u>The Right Thing</u>

I've never been one to be concerned about the consequences that follow from doing the right thing.

Modest Adventures

Modest adventures have the best scenic routes.

<u>Great Things Are Ahead</u>

I suppose I've overdosed on ideas more than a couple of thousand times in my lifetime and, all things considered, am still functioning exceptionally well. I'm busy with projects, and my mind, powered by an unlimited source of inspiration, is still working on overdrive exceeding natural thought limits. I suppose that was a good build up for the punchline, a fairly good verbal drumroll for the climax, and a good preparation paragraph predecessor to the grand finale:

Great Things Are Ahead.

<u>Futures Known By Destiny</u>

There are these fields we cannot see
in these places we cannot be.
Yet we welcome the mystery
in the leaves from each hid tree.
It's true that time holds no space
in which our minds cannot trace.
Yet, oh mystery, we welcome thee
and all the clues that we can see
out there beyond the history
to futures known by destiny.
So we run this narrow race
to that bright and lovely place.
In each season ready, readily
moving forward steady, steadily
with tides turning very quickly
making many worn and sickly.
But not so with us, who see the face
of God's amazing, sustaining grace.

<u>No Place For Gleaning</u>

Your Eyes retrieve me with their gaze
when lies deceive me in their maze.
They set ablaze the spoiled glaze
that causes haze for a phase.
The roaring still above me loud,
the lightning real with its dark cloud.
But howls at night have no more fright,
Your Light is sight, pilots my flight.
Above the storm I set my pace.
Set to perform to win this race.
The old man lagging further behind.
Zigging and zagging, stumbling blind.
So long, old friend. Don't call. Don't write.
You broke at the bend when I went right.
It's okay to die. That's the objective.
There's no eye to eye from either's perspective.
You cannot keep up and you can't maintain.
I emptied your cup in the pouring rain.
I've been washed clean, and though I may splash,
I do not glean in your old trash.
I stir in the glow of a brand new shine.
I row in the flow of a divine design.

Think About It

Don't know about it until you think about it.

Those Types

People who won't admit when they're wrong have no desire to be right.

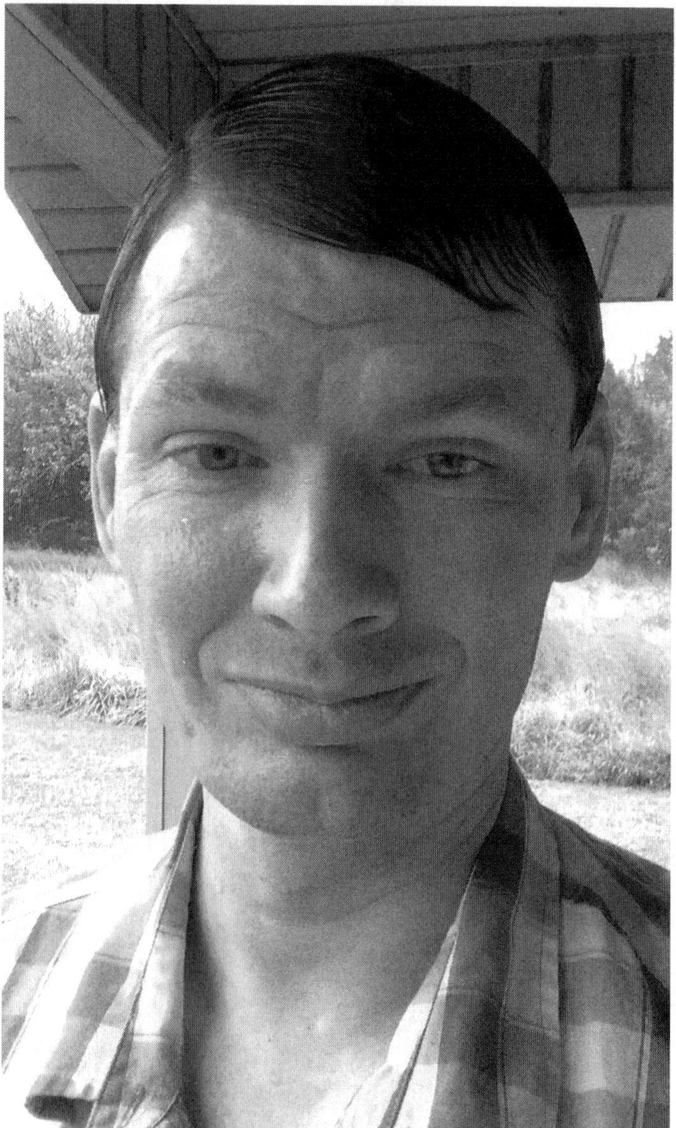

The Future

The future has already happened.

<u>In Effect</u>

I'm not some humdrum bum
in the middle of a slum
with his foot stuck in a gum
holding out a numb thumb.
I'm not some cheat sheet chum
who you can steal life from
like backwoods pond scum
that you hook in your spectrum.

I'm a free tour through the uncharted channels
of the psychological sphere.
I'm a sea of cloudless blue in flight over the surfaces
thinking loud and clear.
The voices of my thoughts teach lessons documented
as the great storms sing.
"The universe in motion with a strong beating heart
preserved by the King."
There is no coin toss at work in these marvelous
wonders we behold.
No luck of the draw at play as these magnificent
moments unfold.
We are in effect like a crystal river never dry
in a plentiful land
roaring like the ocean held safely flowing
in God's firm and mighty Hand.

The End Of The Rainbow

Finding the end of the rainbow can be a difficult task, but not as difficult as finding what we expected to be there.

Expectation

Expectation is the biggest letdown.

<u>Dietary Break Time</u>

The chaos thunders in the disturbed sea
where dishes break in the kitchen's plea.
The key to free the busy bee
will not fit the lazy E.
An effort made needs a minimal C
before that effort can attempt a degree.
But to what does a degree pertain
if the busy bee cannot remain
free?

I Prefer To Be Awake

I would rather be awake continually,
but I go to sleep when I have to.

A Lion Of Righteousness

I am a lion of righteousness that no man can tame.

<u>Ready, Set, Go!</u>

An R is like a star with 18 lots.
An E is like a D with five red dots.
The A stands alone to access a note
the D gets to read from a cloud's boat.
The Y sees the ad for 25 minds.
The S sees an 8 when it rewinds.
The E finds a second place to go
with T and with A as they row the flow.
The G comes in seventh and ninth place,
but O is the star twice ahead in the race.

(I would like for you to try to decipher this poem before I decipher it for you. When you think that you've got it, then read "Deciphering Ready, Set, Go!" to find out whether or not you are correct.)

<u>Deciphering, "Ready, Set, Go!"</u>

The "Ready Set Go" phrase appears after connecting the individual capital letters that are inserted after each line's first word. This is the title of the poem indicating that it's time to start deciphering this complex work, and that it's time for the letters in the poem to begin their race to success.

Line 1. **"An R is like a star with 18 lots."**
Line one's R is like the star letter of this poem, but it isn't the star letter of this poem. The "18 lots" refers to the letter R being the 18th letter in the alphabet, and the word "lots" means "succcsses" as in "successes as a star letter".

Line 2. **"An E is like a D with five red dots."**
Line two's "E is like a D" breaks down into the E being the five (5th letter in the alphabet) and also connects with the D (making it like it) by making the word "RED" from the three single capital letters in lines one and two. The "five red dots" phrase consists of three words that refer to each of the 3 previous capital letters (R.E.D.). The capital R connecting to the scattered word "RED" and also the word "red" in line two, the capital E being the fifth letter in the alphabet, representing the word "five", and the capital D representing the word "dots".

Line 3. "**The A stands alone to access a note**"
Line three's "A" stands alone because it's the first letter of the alphabet, and the word "note" at the end of the line is the "AD" that we see the formation of in line 4. The "A" accesses the note because it's the beginning of the word "AD".

Line 4. "**the D gets to read from a cloud's boat.**"
Line four's "D" completes two words. "AD" and "READ". AD being completed with the capital letters in line's three and four, and READ being completed by the capital letters in lines one through four. The word "note" at the end of line three is referring to the word "AD" and the "D" gets to "read" it (the note/AD) because it's part of the "AD".

Line 5. "**The Y sees the ad for 25 minds.**"
Line five's "Y" sees the ad (AD) for 25 minds. Immediately following the "D" in line four, there are 25 letters completing the rest of the sentence (each letter representing one mind).

Line 6. "**The S sees an 8 when it rewinds.**"
Line six's "S" sees an "8" when it rewinds. If you rewind the alphabet (starting with the letter Z), the letter S is the 8th letter.

Line 7. "**The E finds a second place to go**"
Line seven's "E" finds a second place to go because the letter "E" is the only letter in the phrase "READY SET GO" that appears twice.

Line 8. **"with T and with A as they row the flow."**
Line eight's "T" is with "A" and it's also with "E" from line seven. In their correct order they are ETA, meaning "Estimated Time Of Arrival" which the letters estimate while they "row the flow" which is also a reference to line four's "cloud's boat".

Line 9. **"The G comes in seventh and ninth place,"**
Line nine's "G" comes in seventh place (the seventh letter in the alphabet) and in ninth place (the ninth letter in the phrase READY SET GO). "Place" meaning "in the letters race to be the star letter".

Line 10. **"but O is the star twice ahead in the race."**
Line ten's "O" is the star that's "twice ahead" in the race because the last line is closest to the finish line, indicating that the letter "O" is the most successful letter in the poem, even twice as successful. The "twice ahead" clarifies that even though line nine's "G" placed twice, it's the "O" that's "twice ahead". The "twice ahead" also references back to line one's 18. The "R" related to the 18 because the "R" is the 18th letter in the alphabet. The "O" related to the 18 because the "O" had twice as many successes as the previous 9 letters (2 x 9 = 18). The "R" was like the star letter "O" because "R" started the poem and "O" finished it.

Travels To Destiny

You feel the empty ships as they sail from your eyes
and wonder if their trips will see the friendly skies
as they part from your heart into the chilling breeze
where the tide breaks apart their shadows on the seas
no longer to be heard in the thunder or rain
that kept the early bird from flying through the pain
now eclipsed by a light that's drawn a brand new page
on the sheet of your smile released from its cage.

Your thoughts become more pleasant in the dawn of transparency as they sink their coffins into the void of irrelevancy to bury their dead in the ground of your mentality as the optimistic tree branches to fertility to nurture the forest where spring and fall move rapidly to embrace the whole picture of happenings happily with the revelation that all the pieces fit perfectly in the design of the Master Who created destiny.

The hopeful array fits on your heart very well
as the tailored raiment rings in the welcome bell
that alerts all your senses to the new design
that glistens like the stars with their bright nightly shine
lighting up all the candles in the gray and blue
that illuminate the journey with eyes brand new
that see passed the weather to the clear cloudless sky
through a optical passage in your faith's supply.

Clocks continue with their hands of moments moving steadily across patterns of the temporal and the perpetually instilled to transpire into the purposed reality that's revealed eventually in the seekers inquiry at that time when mortality puts on immortality and the brightened day remains forever in eternity when existence crosses over into a spiritual country where the divinely guided roads meet in the blissful heavenly.

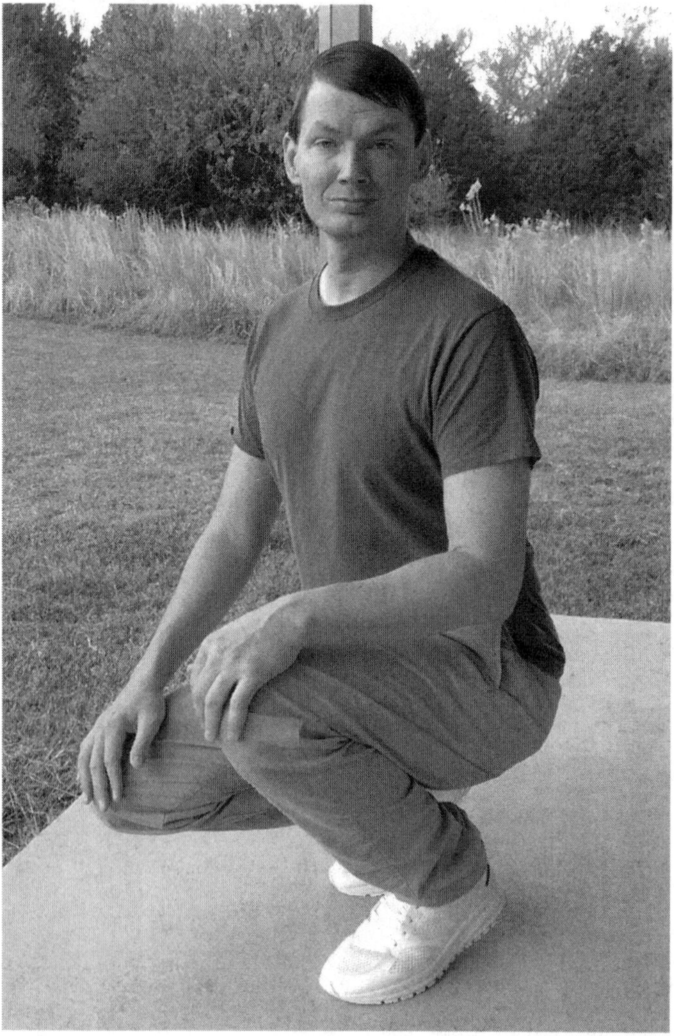

Used To It

I'm used to criticism, but I'm also used to being right.

The Annals Of Endeavors

Night cliffs, what ifs
are pulsating like a crash
through dots like thoughts
of equating cash with trash.

Dark scene, no screen
to hinder what you feel
inside the tide
where many drowned their will.

Green greed, false need
of desired tangible treasures
mean faced, misplaced
in the annals of endeavors.

Sad fears, cold tears
in touch with letting go
of dreams, night screams
outsourced by your ego.

Here now somehow
is a moment you can see
without one doubt
of how things need to be.

One foot stays put
while the other lifts in air
to reach the breach
of all your life's despair.

You make, not break,
with a step off the right cliff
where you rise new
up above the what if stiff.

You're soaring, not pouring,
and the way you lift your head
is classic, so graphic,
like a nightlight glowing red.

Faith saves from graves
that thought-shovels like to dig
in minds like blinds
kept down from thinking big.

But now somehow
a sky window's caught your eye,
and that format
is why you chose to fly.

A Friendly Storm

You open up your days with portals of gold
overlapping the rays with treasures on hold
to standby while you wait for the storms to pass
over your sweet home plate beside of your glass
that breaks when the lightning strikes a "see" chord
when the strings start tightening the right vocal cord
that tries to thunder in on optimism
like a friend with a spin on activism
that says, "your ambition is limiting you
by cost of admission, your own I.O.U.
in the well you wish in to feel more content
in the life you fish in to bill what you've spent
and call it investments in a future place
where all your assessments are kept in a brace."

The memories at that time will be whirlwinds of wrecks where you will always wind up in better shape than in your, then, present condition where you will consider the pleasantries that you never partook of due to your continual reach into a future cookie jar that turned out to be a mouse trap with a aftershock that has the ability to keep you caved in on the bottom floor of your collapsed mental edifice that you unknowingly constructed to be explosive in the hometown pennies of your dwelling.

The towels are looking sweet in your ring of tears,
a million packed up neat for your future years,
to be tossed in portals now shown to all hold
the vain dreams of mortals that wilt with the gold
so often sought after while bypassing hearts
that beat in the laughter where happiness starts
like an engine with keys that read all the maps
now deciding the breeze won't bridge to collapse
because the mystery of its direction
reveals a history of reconnection
and in that history waits something brand new,
beyond the sophistry, a path that is true,
and that fine line is set in just the right place
to avoid every net that's tossed in the race.

The transparent dim glow brightens down the halls of your social distancing and you begin to draw closer to the shunned faces you had been taught to avoid for the cheaper cost of your future that is now embraced in the circumference of daily perimeters rather than in aspired decades of wishful thinking where the pinnacle of those thoughts desensitized the joys of the journey to the point of nullifying the here and now which has now been miraculously resuscitated by a friendly storm.

Pensive Penny

Pensive Penny took a penny from out her pail
then Pensive Penny tossed that penny into the well
where plenty pennies, thought as Genies, all had fell.
Then Pensive Penny left for twenty days to tell
if that penny was the penny that would prevail
to be the penny unlike the many from her pail,
which hadn't any other pennies for the well.
But after the twenty day penny timescale,
Pensive Penny found that penny also to fail.
Pensive Penny had tossed that penny to no avail.

So Pensive Penny took the penny from her
penny loafer's penny holder,
then Pensive Penny held up that penny, which
was shinier and older,
and on bended knee took then she the penny
from her other penny loafer's penny holder,
then Pensive Penny, standing bolder, with no
penny in either penny loafer penny holder,
tossed both pennies over her shoulder.

<u>Pensive Penny And Gullible Gail</u>

Pensive Penny, with no penny had she,
walked up to the well.
Then Pensive Penny, with wits aplenty,
kicked over her friend's pail.
"There's no penny like a Genie," said she
to Gullible Gail.
"Not any in the many," Pensive Penny
came to tell.
Gullible Gail took not that well,
but listened all the same.
Of coins that fell, she'd hoped one would
prevail in bringing her acclaim.
So Gullible Gail looked at her pail,
and the coins about its frame,
then presumptions fell as Gullible Gail
looked high to take new aim.

<u>Pensive Penny And Wishful Whitney</u>

Pensive Penny knew Wishful Whitney
had a penny in her hand.
So Pensive Penny did not tarry,
but ran she out on the sand.
Pensive Penny beat Wishful Whitney
to the well across the land.
Then Pensive Penny spread out widely
her arms and legs as planned
to keep Wishful Whitney from tossing her penny
into a la-la land.
Wishful Whitney marveled plenty
at the red head pert and tanned.
How necessary was this unordinary
display of command?
Pensive Penny, with white shirt dusty,
stood firmly in her stand.
The freckly girly in denim shorts, pretty,
caught her breath to myths disband.
She told Wishful Whitney that hope in a penny
was merely sinking sand.
But Wishful Whitney knew a well and a penny
went traditionally hand in hand.

Could Pensive Penny make Wishful Whitney
truly understand
that a well and a penny did not in reality
go so hand in hand?

Initially Wishful Whitney wanted to knock Pensive Penny
right out of her penny loafers.
To knock her silly, then ground pound her deeply
to keep company with the gophers.

But Pensive Penny let up not any and was able to explain
that no penny was like a Genie, and it was faith that
would sustain.
And eventually dusty Pensive Penny rubbed off on
Wishful Whitney, who put her only penny back into
her pocket.
And a deeply relieved Pensive Penny then added
Wishful Whitney, metaphorically, to her heart's locket.

<u>Thwart The Cruel Intentions</u>

Don't brood in the recoils of your efforts.
Don't come apart in your apprehensions.
Take a deep breath, and relax your thoughts.
You can thwart all of the cruel intentions.
Devise a strategy to maneuver
out of the perilous devices
that the devious like to construct
to cut off your distinguished advices.
Concentrate and then deactivate
the timer that is set to explode
the rational intellectual mind
that cannot be traded, bought or sold.

Take leaps of thought to new measures to the distances that bypass the common monumental phenomenals to the uncharted waters now required to expand their perimeters in order to accommodate the cognitive guest, with the new fashion in critical thinking, so to appropriately make the journey a pleasant one for this new type of psychological voyager that has materialized in the cerebral sphere.

Break through all the chains of their deceit.
Steady your hands and steady your feet.
They like to bite and they like to cheat.
Don't let them drowned out your heart's neat beat.
See beyond the surface of what you view.
Look deeper than what your mind's used to.
Don't get clenched in their teeth where they chew.
Don't get drenched in the lies that they spew.
Be fixed like a torpedo rocket.
Stay plugged in like a lamp in a socket.
Don't get picked like guitars in a pocket.
Display your mind like a opened locket.

Don't allow them to curb your intellect or to put a curfew on your thoughts as though to dictate your reasoning so that it can't pull up the curtain on their act meant to short-circuit the wires connected to the heart of your conscience where the light that they fear is too bright for their eyes to maintain their travels in the night across the stage of their programmed applause where they toil in their vanity.

<u>Poetic</u>

Beauty dawns in the winged day
soaring through beams of bright array
fitted in destinies on display
with smiling thoughts to convey.
No ocean drowns in our hearts
filled with the towns of early starts
far from the cities where they part
like troubled seas that won't kickstart.
Efforts don't just bloom on their own
as if they were coded to work alone.
A kite needs wind for it to be flown,
and a life needs wind that's Spirit blown.
We are sustained through the cycle rides
over the mountains and even the tides.
Our beautiful memories do abide
of the many lit paths led by our Guide.
The flowered trails through blossomed fields.
No broken sails or voyage yields.
The poetic heights, therein revealed
the transparent sights, no more concealed.

Merging streams flow as one tree
branching to engulf each thirsty plea
desiring the fullness of the sea
where faith steps out to take the key.
Doors unlocking that never could swim
suddenly knocking on the deepest rim.
The bells are ringing in a new hymn
as the courts all stand in the golden gym.
The sun illuminates each reaching joy.
Neighbor sees neighbor and no decoy.
A divine unit of hope to deploy.
A lovely celestial convoy.

Illuminated Destinies

We shipwreck ourselves beneath stars of hope
enriched with the notions we cannot cope
with all the many dreams that never came true
at the end of the sagas where they broke into
a million pieces that we wanted to be
pieced together in our reality,
but to that end had they no substance to cohere,
and broke they instead like a fallen chandelier.

The map is detailed in the suburbs of our intellect leading to prosperous confines of contentment designated for our benefit superseding the fabrications of materialistic dreamlands constructed with infamous preconceptions of fulfillment, never aligning with the hype, that tended to deep pocket the moral compass known for keeping ships afloat.

The pennies fell with the stars as we waited
for hindsight to catch up to the contemplated
as we stood by for the best only to find
the best was in danger of being left behind
in a shallow grave that we thought was a shot
at getting the riches that all too soon rot
like a sacred apple not meant to be eaten
by reckless ambitions that get egos beaten.

We grow as we die in the light of maturity while simultaneously developing a eternal character that blossoms in heaven's celestial fields as we partake of a divine nature that establishes our place among the royal ancestry proceeding with perpetual gratitude of the pierced Hands that keep us together, separated from the darkness that has no properties in our illuminated destinies.

Barefoot Walks

Domino effects ripple across the ocean
as their happenings instill thoughts like a potion
with the good, the bad, and the ugly ducklings
crossing their border roads with smirks and chucklings
while the transpired remains true to the best
revealed at the end of the rainbow as a test
passed in the straight lanes where the devout all drive
as the wide world of unsportsmanship deprive
themselves from the joys of the journey
as their masks keep their lives on a gurney.

These foiled rings get answered in the twilight when the price isn't right for the cost of the guilt quilted in the wide lake where the ugly thoughts quack on the darkening clock that sets the pace for their drownings in the shallow waters of their murky ambitions unable to find the fish and loaves where the devout got their fill at the station where the flight was on board with the train of thought on the right track.

The faces on the palms brighten in the storm
as painful surges reveal a future that's warm
where the palm trees don't grow in their dirty deeds
that branched into crimes of various breeds
that attacked the voyagers who rode the sharks
through midnights and noons in jungles and parks
never to lose sight of the relaxed barefoot walks
in the grass of accomplishment where wisdom talks
as the gentle sounds of thunder are understood,
in the transparent rain, as times that were good.

So much is taken for granted in the travels that build the fountains that nourish the future gardens where the scent of the roses is consistent with the tide of hope that is continual in the destination dawnings that often aren't detected until the clock comes back into focus and is recognized as a treasure rather than as a self-fabricated burden waiting to be recycled in the embrace of its long awaited distance.

Enter The Exit

We shatter in painful images
that reflect back on our broken dreams
while searching for lines of scrimmages
to hold back the inward screams.
But ducks have a way of quacking
beneath the surface of breath
and bucks have a way of backtracking
in the movement that leads to death.
So putting voices on hold
may prolong insanity's ride,
but when it comes time to fold,
there isn't a place to hide.
So we move like a wilderness
in these trees that leave us in the wind,
branching to prove a yielder's fitness
doesn't retrieve a mend.
The fine tuning of our minds
is sometimes like a best guess.
We aim to straighten the winds
by playing ourselves at chess.
We turn like TVs on standby
dialing channels that ingest
the pockets that hold our hands dry
while manuals have time to digest.

Our laboring for relief
isn't always so neat and dry.
But inside our core belief
are the wings that can take us high.
We fly to turn the tide, we try
to breathe and not to backtrack
to the place that crashes the sky
into fields where panics attack.
We seek to find these buzz puzzles
that sting, but never connect
life's guzzles to life's muzzles—
the effect, a v-necked turtle wrecked.
A fancy shell of torment
unbuttoned to bear the cold
that should be locked and dormant,
instead of parked to be strolled.
These sights aren't fixed, nor set in stone,
our points of view can surely change.
Our time is worth the wait alone,
if that wait's to rearrange
our broken steps with truths of gold
that radiate a celestial day,
the old to new, the new to bold,
as we finally say, "NO WAY!"

We won't be dressed in tatters,
in rags that wipe our fuel out.
We'll move the piece that matters
until passed the cesspool drought.
We'll see with our own two clearing eyes
the big blur that caused vexation,
and we'll cross our legs while in the skies
as the mind finds its relaxation.
Clarity will shine true throughout
as the dismal clouds depart,
and things we used to stress about
will calm down inside the heart.
Our glimmers will ring once again
as the dial tone gets through
and the calls we make will let us in
through the door of something new.
The exit won't need a sign to stand
by the road of sweat and decay.
We've grasped the Hand that made this land,
and this place is where we'll stay.

Poetic Cognition

So what is poetry? Poetry is a representation of the heart, fashioned by the mind. There are divers styles, classifications, and levels of poetry, each signifying a difference in the relevance to creativity. There are things that can be taught, and then there are things that have to be known. Poetry has to be known. Poetry isn't about mimicking, copying, or imitating, it's about being and being original. Poetry isn't complicated to the poet, and it's not impossible for the illiterate.

Illiteracy is merely a step that the illiterate never took, but the step is still there like so many steps are. There are lots of steps never taken in life, and many lives are struggling at the bottom of their self-induced handicaps. It's amazing what steps can do, and even the ones broken can be mended. Poetry is there to be written, explored, and examined, but never mimicked. The mirror is not poetry, the sky is.

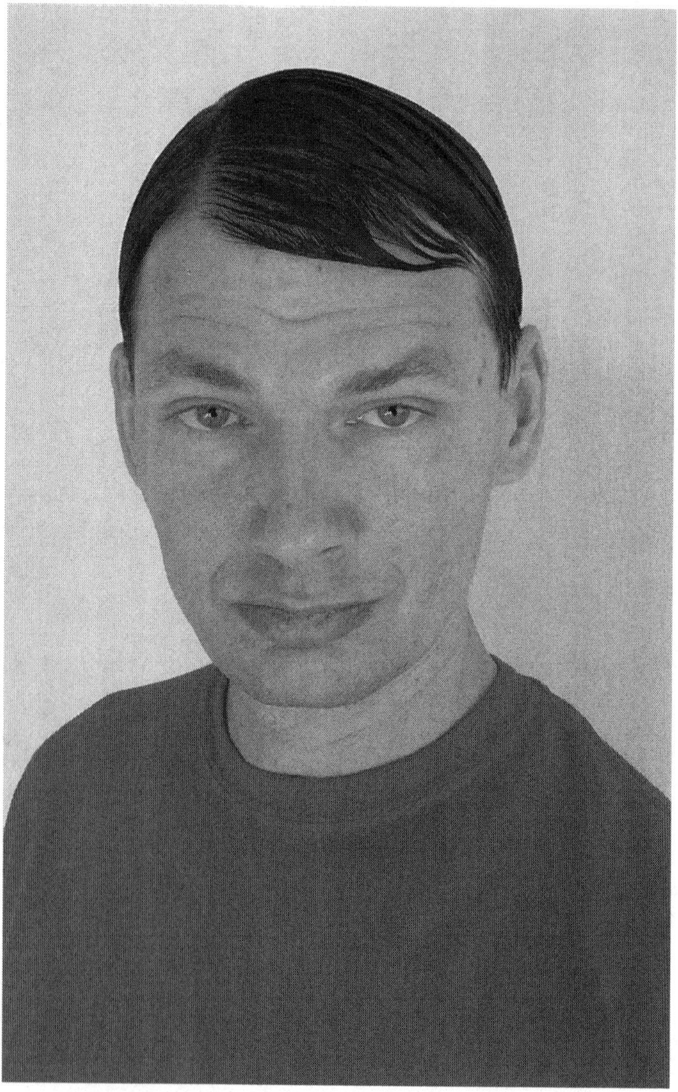

About the Author

Calvin W. Allison was born in a town called Ada in the state of Oklahoma.

When he was four years of age, his family moved from the town of Ada to a remote location deep in the country where he grew up. His immediate biological family consisted of himself, his dad, mom, and two sisters.

The years passed while the surrounding climate of his childhood took him through the diverse seasons of growth where the developing cycles of character took their effect. During his 7th to 10th grade years at the educational edifice called school, he experienced some very difficult times that caused his emotions to darken, and his self-esteem to sink low into the dimly lit hallways of manic depression. Inward hurt outwardly resulted in a reckless living that sent him staggering to find balance down a pathway obstructed with self-constructed landmines that he narrowly edged his way around. During that dark venturing (while in self-destruct mode) he wrote numerous volumes of negative poetry, and surrounded his life with dark secular entertainment that intensified his excessive impulses for erosion. He attached himself to harmful habits, often indulging in drug use, and in alcoholic consumption. As a result of his dangerous addictions, he went off-road into several ditches, encountered various perils, and once spent a night in a physical jail. The time that he spent existing was unproductive, and the chains of the world were steadily tightening around his vague hope of progressing. Though the rope of his unstableness was long enough to stretch through an accumulation of scarred up years, it reached its end on the night of February 7th 1999. On that night he stepped away from the toxic waste that he had become, and toward the belief that there was Someone there that could help him. So he called out to God with a sincere heart, and then received an experience that gave him an unyielding desire to continue seeking God. Then one night he opened up his heart and received Jesus Christ as his Lord and Savior.

Calvin was born again, and everything in his life became brand new. His eyes were opened up, and he could see things with a spiritual clarity that he had previously been unable to. His perspective on life completely changed, and he got rid of all the negative volumes of poetry that he had written. He also got rid of all the dark secular entertainment that had once contributed to his condition of grief. The light of God's pure redeeming truth had filled his heart and mind with a love that reconstructed his entire being.

Now Calvin writes for the glory of God, and bears witness to the life changing Gospel of Jesus Christ.

Calvin is a well learned student of the Bible who stands strong in the faith of the Lord. He is a Conservative American with a good understanding of the political system, and he has an interest in the field of true science. His Christian values are the foundation of any subject that he advances in, and upon that foundation he cannot be moved. Whether the subjects are of political significance , scientific significance , or of any other subjects of significance, Calvin strongly believes that they must be proven durable from a Biblical standpoint. If they cannot be proven durable from a Biblical standpoint, then he believes that they have no place in the classifications that are relevant to importance, and therefore have no underlined substance to offer that would be beneficial to anyone.

Calvin is proficient in writing in various forms of styles, including in a second person format, as was demonstrated in this short documentation of biographical/ testimonial information.

He hopes that his books greatly bless everyone who reads them.

Also Available From Calvin W. Allison:

Joan (a poem/short story)
A Sunset Rising
A Peace in the Spirit
Shadows Over February
Growing in the Presence of God
Standing at the Top of the Hill
Strong Love Church
The Sunset of Science and the Risen Son of Truth